WHAT TH
TAUGH

C000091486

What the House Taught Us

Poems by Anne Bailey

THE EMMA PRESS

First published in the UK in 2021 by The Emma Press Ltd.
Poems © Anne Bailey 2021.

ISBN 978-1-912915-91-0

A CIP catalogue record of this book
is available from the British Library.

Printed and bound in the UK
by the Holodeck, Birmingham.

The Emma Press
theemmapress.com
hello@theemmapress.com
Birmingham, UK

CONTENTS

Going off and other kinds of default

In the early stages you can't see if milk has soured:
it could have turned and gone completely
before you got a smell of its departure.

Meat can go bad. This delinquency at least
can be detected by the smell,
but no remedial action will be effective.

Grain, vegetables and fruit are spoilers:
overnight whole harvests can rot.
This conspiracy is easily seen by the naked eye.

Things that dry out from the inside
are hardest to deal with: disintegration
leaves no trace until it is too late.

An egg, for example, can look like a good egg
even after its contents have been blown.
A walnut could be black and empty when cracked.

You wouldn't know until you put your foot on its shell
whether the snail was a danger to the cabbage.
You wouldn't know if anyone was waiting at home
until you opened the door.

I stare up at the house

It is made of stone: large blocks
of Millstone Grit. Strange this strength,
this protection I don't remember.

These walls moved in the wind
so at night the beds shifted their feet,
the windows closed their eyes,

the tiles on the roof
gossiped about the birds
which never stayed for long.

These walls were curved.
They crumbled the way
stuffing comes out of cushions,

or a carpet frays,
or the table has one short leg
causing drinks to spill,

or a cinder falls on the hearthrug,
to smoulder unseen
until it catches a throat.

Sudden death

The father clasps the child's hands
and spins around until her feet leave the ground.

Her arms almost come out of their sockets
but she shrieks with pleasure.

A short time later he dies;
this is when he lets her go

but the child continues to fly. She resists
all attempts to bring her down.

The problem with magic

There was a place on the third step down
near the top of the stairs where a child
was invisible. This is where the girl stood

one afternoon when she was four years old
and her father had gone out, leaving her,
her brother and her mother alone in the house.

There was a knock at the door and it was not a Fox,
or a Troll, or a Wolf. It was her grandmother
with the news of her father's death.

There was a moment, there on the step, when she knew
that special powers were hers if she chose them.
She gripped the handrail and turned to go

back up the stairs where she made a promise
to her baby brother asleep in his cot: *I will make sure
that evil will not befall us for the rest of our lives.*

There was the thrill of standing tall and strong,
and through the window, the warmth
of the rays of the sun.

There is a mind in which this girl exists,
still holding up the sky. It has never occurred to her
that she could have chosen to cry.

When the lake came

it occupied a space in the living room
between the sofa and the fireplace.

It kept very still, made no demands,
showed a perfect reflection of the lamp on the table.

It was an inconvenience
we had to stop the children from jumping in.

Eventually they understood: *We walk round it,*
avoid staring, get on with our lives.

I think of it as deep and cold;
there are hints of a breeze but no smell.

It has a magnetic pull.
We lean towards it as we pass,

shoot a glance in its direction
hoping no one else notices.

Is it getting bigger? Is it awake?
Is that a breeze, a whiff of something?

What would happen if we leaned over
and looked right in?

Concern for Mother

It was when the tail poked out of her ear
the family became alarmed,
though they didn't like to mention it.

I mean, how could you say:
*Mum, what's that? It looks like the tail
of a mouse.* (*Or rat*, said Jack.)

She was just the same apart from that;
didn't seem to feel the twitch
as it curled, twisted at the tip

then disappeared – and there behind her eyes:
a button nose and a rush of fur,
whiskers in the other ear.

*Oh Mum, sit you down, take the weight
off your feet. Have some tea.*

What I learnt about men

Aunt Edith had a lot to answer for. She was a witch with a mole on the end of her nose and lips like a crushed lemon, or a serpent with a flicked-out tongue, or the Virgin Mary keeping her legs crossed all the time. She was married to the organist who was LIKE A STICK IN BED, before capitulating to the piano tuner. Claiming it was ONLY THE ONCE didn't cut it, did not give her licence to throw down tablets of stone and rain on everybody else's picnic.

Aunt Vera had a sad life. When her husband died she went out AND GOT ANOTHER MAN and it didn't matter that when she laughed her bosoms bounced up and down – she had to look after him for years and him coughing up phlegm everywhere, taking a long time to die.

Aunt Ella was STRONGER THAN SHE LOOKED, like birds are strong but will break – especially if they live in a house no one is allowed to visit with a man who has tattoos and a broken nose from fighting and children with ordinary names like Andrew but strange illnesses that mean they can't attend school.

Aunt Irene liked the good life. Bingo, dancing; she even jived down the Working Men's Club on a Saturday, but she was hampered by APPEARANCES as Frank was the spitting image of Alan Ladd, meaning anybody would have gone for him, not noticing the signs. He was a man who could hold his beer, which is eventually mostly all he did.

Dinky the budgerigar

His last flight into scalding water from the tap
was his mistake, but my mother blamed herself.
I made him a bed from a clean orange duster,
the softest cloth, in a shoebox for him to rest:
regain his exotic plumage of pure emerald green
crowned with speckled ermine.

But you can't save a bird: its legs, its neck
once broken do not mend like ours.
After a fall it is already halfway out of its skin,
as if the root of each feather were a perforation.
I didn't know that then, but it was Sunday,
Whitsun, a good day to pray.

The thin elastic on my chapel hat cut into my skin:
those hats, so much sunshine on the long faced pews,
a new coat straight from the box, the smell of polyester,
chiffon scarves, lipstick, men with shining shoes,
a Festival, just to be there and want something
so very much. It should have been enough.

Beyond these things

There is no god.
There is no house
but the walls and the roof.

I sit on the front doorstep
to revise Latin grammar.
I recite declensions.

There is a bird in the chimney –
hear its repeated panic.
My mother's panic is worse.

I can catch the sun
on my arms and legs,
my back against rough stone.

A jackdaw falls into the grate;
the soot will be trodden
into the carpet, the clean sheets.

I tilt my head right back;
the sun pours into my face
until it scorches my skin.

On the radio Procul Harum
are top of the pops with
'A Whiter Shade of Pale'.

There are black wing marks
on the bedroom wall.
This sort of dirt never comes out.

The little girl and the universe

A man watches a little girl
push her doll's pram with determination
up the steep path at the side of her house.
It comes to a stop at a step.

Not being aware of the laws of physics
that dictate she would have to push down
on the handle in order to continue her journey,
she bashes the pram repeatedly against the step.

The man, seeing a role for himself,
strides over and bends down to help,
not being aware that until he came along
the problem had been a relatively simple one.

Mind's eye

There is a place in a wood,
in the bottom of a drawer,
at the back of a mind.

A disused quarry in which
men cut stone from a hillside,
ground it into slabs, carted it away

leaving a precipice hidden
in the undergrowth:
a sheer drop of eighty feet,

a chasm filled with water
deep as the pit in your stomach,
cold as a last breath,

still as a sightless eye.
Cousin Brenda's mother,
Arthur's second wife, was found

bloated and floating there
in nineteen eighty-two.
It's not the sort of thing

you often think about,
not somewhere you would
ever want to go.

For the record

Because we continued   to write it all
down   because we remembered
not letting anything go unnoticed at
least at first   because we knew a
certain amount   enough to   feel
superior in some ways   we rehearsed
it   until it became a song   with
verses and a   refrain which we
heard repeated but badly   so that
children   went   missing   and
sometimes   were   substituted.
People got the wrong   end of the stick
went looking in   damp places
lost their heads   so that for a long
time things went   backwards   there
seemed to be   no end to it   even
the middle gave way   perforated by
worship   and a certain kind of
celebration   which because
we wrote it all down we remembered

My mother

is a coat I wear most of the time.
It has no buttons but lots of pockets

(In one is *The Black and White Minstrels*,
Ken Dodd and *Songs of Praise*.)

The lining is overstitched with brand names:
Player's, 99 Tea, Swan Vestas.

The coat is made of wool but it scratches my skin;
causes open mouthed wounds that bleat

complaints about the way things do not
very often turn out for the best.

I might be inundated by nicotined excuses,
ambushed by mugs of hot, strong cries for help.

I might wake up to find all the novels
of Jeffrey Archer stacked in my throat.

I would take it off but there is no doubt
it has some warmth: the collar for example

knows a thing or two, especially about
Mrs Butterworth and how she thinks she is better

than everybody else though we all know
she never married Mr Butterworth

and anyway not all of the children are his,
or what Miriam gets up to in the office

to impress the boss, or in the war what happened
to posh women when they joined up,

or how to tap dance in a sailor's suit
and when to sing a song backwards.

How to get the most out of baking

Put butter in a baking bowl,
set it in front of the fire, then
call up the dead.

Watch your grandmother cream
sugar into butter with a small fork,
the bowl in her lap.

Notice the spare skin on her face
wobble with the effort, the set of her mouth,
the strength in her hand.

Feel the house settle around her,
the fire penetrate; see the pattern on her legs
from its friendly damage.

As she straightens to walk into the kitchen
to find the scales, the eggs and the flour,
switch off your food mixer.

Domestic

So you've put a picture on the lovely blank wall

that used to go pink in the sun
and feel like an ice cream.

A wall on which I used to rest my eyes
in pleasant contemplation.

A wall which represented air
that could be breathed.

A wall through which it was possible to see
how much space is in the universe.

The distance between one star and another.

The sum of the parts

Felicity was wooded. Her open spaces were full of damp washing, mostly in piles but some strewn around, aspiring to dryness. Her skyline was erratic. She spent most of her time responding to alerts. She couldn't rely on the undergrowth and even at night the birds sang.

Nigel was tarmacked, with a central reservation but no hard shoulder. He worried about fumes but had become dependent on straight lines. He kept a lookout for cracks on the surface: abrasions, open wounds. He wanted to relax into a different week, one with not so many eyeballs and no smell of burning.

Guy was already instagrammed, fully screened and adequately covered in every setting. His wallpaper was stubbled. Notifications required the reflex action of only one thumb. Nevertheless, connections were trembled by the proximity of real skin or the gaze from an actual eye.

Lizzie's door was open but she was still inside counting the pencils and wondering if the balloons had had enough to eat. Her cupboards were full of snow-covered forests, which was a big responsibility, let alone what would happen to the bears if she ever left.

The family turned itself inside out and walked upside down if it had to. It learnt tricks, could juggle with five balls whilst jumping through a hoop. It practised going in one direction and if it ever got to the top of the hill all it ever wanted to do was come down again. It counted itself obsessively and was extremely nervous about the lions.

I Was Struck By Lightning While Ironing

Headline in the Times, *13.6.20*

It was when I had got to that very tricky part on a man's shirt up near the collar, round the top button on the left-hand side. I had already finished the back; watched the steam billow out as all the creases gave way under pressure, the plate of the iron through the strength of my arm, forcing a way, unstoppable. The joy of this power, like shaving all the hair off a person's head or ploughing a field. Whatever does not get moulded into shape the first time succumbs on the return. Anyway, I was really having to concentrate, pushing the nose right down to get at all the creases, and just when I had got it exactly how I wanted it there was a loud bang. Everything stopped. The iron, stationary now, rested on the shirt, causing a lethal scorch the exact shape and size of the plate, slightly above the left breast.

Uses and abuses of the tea towel

It would be acceptable to mop up spilt milk with a tea towel but best not to clean shoes with it or actually mop the floor.

The towel should be ironed after washing to kill germs and kept in a prominent and accessible place in the kitchen.

Tea towels can display certain information like:
How to Peel a Carrot
A map of Lincolnshire
Wild Flowers of England
and slogans such as, *Life is Fantastic.*

A tea towel can serve as a sling for a sprained wrist or hold a packet of peas against a sore neck. When flicked in an expert fashion it can kill a blow fly or annoy a dog.

A wet tea towel can be used to stifle flames in an overheated deep fat fryer.

The corner of a tea towel with spit on it is good at getting the speck out of someone's eye.

A tea towel is what you will use to save the life of the bird flown in by mistake and now trapped in your kitchen.

Did she prefer life as a door?

after Jane Monson

She started off as a daisy of course,
then downgraded to a dandelion,
then a plant pot. Being a pencil was OK,
but by the time she was a level crossing,
having not stayed as a signpost for very long,
life felt heavy, like when she was an aircraft carrier,
and even though there was a period of time
as a crystal ball she became a drainpipe,
then a dustbin. Now she was afraid.
She pondered the extent to which a door
could inflict injury on herself or others,
the impossibility of knowing what lay behind it,
what the direction of travel should be.

A film of dust is how it starts

The planet rubs its back on the curve
of space; its crust disintegrates bit by bit.

Which is a form of letting things go:
dirty plates in the sink, a pile of ironing,
not setting the table, unshaven legs.

Which is just the kind of mess
microbes and fungi thrive in:
break down remains, recycle the dead.

Which is where they live now in soil
along with worms and roots of trees:
creating their own cities, motorways, canals.

Which is good for the planet,
keeping it warm, all in one piece,
spinning out there on its own.

Which worked for a long time,
but you could say it should not have slept
so long in its fleece-lined coat.

Which has resulted in some overproduction:
leaving the kettle on to boil,
not turning off the bath taps, smoking in bed.

Which is another way of saying people grew out
    of the Earth:
went to town, had a party, used all the deodorant,
threw the tea leaves down the sink.

Which means there are so many tea leaves
down the sink the microbes are inundated;
they can't cope. Something will have to be done.

The Curator is married to the rain

1.

Things aren't always easy.
There are exhibits in his museum
which need his attention:
a spot of paint here, oil there,
a screw that must be tightened.
Sometimes it feels as if he is
more Creator than Curator.

Rain has mood swings
and he isn't always there
to catch her when she falls,
or perhaps she falls
because he isn't there.
She has become preoccupied
with thoughts of this.

Talk to me, she says.
You are my only love, he says.
I feel alone, she says.
I keep you in my heart, he says.
I can't live in a glass case, she says.
He looks at her as if
he has never seen her before.

2.

The Curator is hard at work.
Rain notices his little grunts,
the intensity in the way he swallows.

She realises he is coming to the end
of a project and wonders what
the implications of this will be.

*I have put all the saucepans
in this drawer*, he says, *but the lids
need to be stacked neatly along the front.*

That should make things a lot easier for you.
Rain does not want to dampen his spirits
too much today, so she smiles

to give him some encouragement.
I am prepared to give it a try, she says.

3.

The trouble is,
now that the Curator is ill
it is all about him.

He is methodical,
single minded. He packs
what he needs

for the hospital
carefully, takes
his innermost thoughts

which are already folded
and pushes them down
firmly into his overnight bag.

Rain is secretly pleased;
it confirms everything
she knows about him.

He looks up. A door
in his gaze has been left open.
Things inside are all at sea.

Where are the glass-fronted
certainties, the carefully-spaced
bones of contention?

This devastation is my doing,
she thinks. *It has my mark on it.*

4.

But really the Curator and Rain are both balloons –
you can decide on the colour.

Rain feels resentful because the Curator seems unaware
of her existence. She has to prod him

to make things happen but the reason he doesn't move
very far or very fast is because he has to concentrate.

He is sitting on the string attached to Rain
to keep her safe. For him it is an act of love.

ACKNOWLEDGEMENTS

Thanks are due to the editors of *Under the Radar, Lighthouse, Ink Sweat and Tears, Brittle Star* and *Obsessed with Pipework* where some of these poems first appeared.

Thanks also to the brilliant tutors from whom I learnt and am continuing to learn my craft: Julia Webb, Helen Ivory, Agnieszka Studzinska, Jacqueline Saphra and the Poetry School for providing the inspiring courses that generated many of these poems.

I thank the members of my Norwich poetry group, my Poetry School writing group and my Stanza group, especially Ramona Herdman who helped to edit this pamphlet, and all the community of poets in and around Norwich who have been vital to the publication of my work.

I am grateful to Emma Wright for choosing to publish this pamphlet, for her design skills and unfailing positivity which made the whole project a real adventure.

ABOUT THE POET

Anne Bailey is a Yorkshirewoman now living and writing poetry in North Norfolk. She has worked as a teacher, a mother and a couples counsellor in London. She is a committee member for Café Writers, organising poetry events in Norwich. Her poem 'What the River did Next' was commended in the 2021 Ambit Poetry Competition.

You can find her on Twitter: @Anneebai

ABOUT THE EMMA PRESS

The Emma Press is an independent publishing house based in the Jewellery Quarter, Birmingham, UK. It was founded in 2012 by Emma Dai'an Wright, and specialises in poetry, short fiction and children's books.

The Emma Press has been shortlisted for the Michael Marks Award for Poetry Pamphlet Publishers in 2014, 2015, 2016, 2018, and 2020, winning in 2016.

In 2020 The Emma Press received funding from Arts Council England's Elevate programme, developed to enhance the diversity of the arts and cultural sector by strengthening the resilience of diverse-led organisations.

Website: theemmapress.com
Facebook, Twitter and Instagram:
@TheEmmaPress